DiscoverRoo
An Imprint of Pop!
popbooksonline.com

HISTORY'S SPOOKIEST PARANORMAL EVENTS

by Grace Hansen

abdobooks.com

Published by Pop!, a division of ABDO, PO Box 398166, Minneapolis, Minnesota 55439. Copyright © 2023 by Abdo Consulting Group, Inc. International copyrights reserved in all countries. No part of this book may be reproduced in any form without written permission from the publisher. DiscoverRoo™ is a trademark and logo of Pop!.

Printed in the United States of America, North Mankato, Minnesota.

052022
092022

THIS BOOK CONTAINS RECYCLED MATERIALS

Cover Photos: Shutterstock Images; Alamy
Interior Photos: Shutterstock Images; Getty Images; Library of Congress

Editor: Elizabeth Andrews
Series Designer: Candice Keimig; Laura Graphenteen

Library of Congress Control Number: 2021951840
Publisher's Cataloging-in-Publication Data

Names: Hansen, Grace, author.

Title: History's spookiest paranormal events / by Grace Hansen

Description: Minneapolis, Minnesota : Pop, 2023 | Series: History's greatest mysteries | Includes online resources and index

Identifiers: ISBN 9781098242312 (lib. bdg.) | ISBN 9781098243012 (ebook)

Subjects: LCSH: Ghosts--Juvenile literature. | Metaphysics (Parapsychology)--Juvenile literature. | Curiosities and wonders--Juvenile literature.

Classification: DDC 130--dc23

WELCOME TO DiscoverRoo!

Pop open this book and you'll find QR codes loaded with information, so you can learn even more!

Scan this code* and others like it while you read, or visit the website below to make this book pop!

popbooksonline.com/paranormal-events

*Scanning QR codes requires a web-enabled smart device with a QR code reader app and a camera.

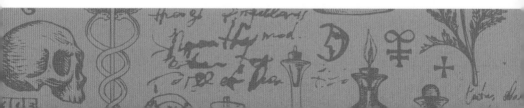

TABLE OF
CONTENTS

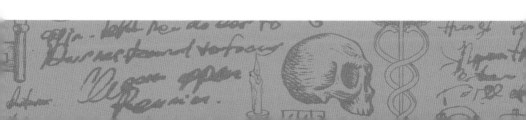

CHAPTER 1

WHAT COMES NEXT?

People have always wondered what comes after life. Some groups believe **souls** go to happy places, like a heaven. Others think spirits keep living around us. Sometimes this can be due to tragic circumstances that left the dead trapped

WATCH A VIDEO HERE!

In Greek Mythology, Charon carried the souls of the dead across the river Styx to the gates of the underworld.

on Earth. And still others believe that souls

are reborn into new bodies. The answers

could be found in one of these **theories**,

or perhaps there is truth in all of them.

CHAPTER 2

GETTYSBURG'S GHOSTS

July 1, 1863, marked the start of one of

the deadliest battles on American soil.

Toward the end of the **Civil War**, Union

and Confederate forces fought for three

days in Gettysburg, Pennsylvania, until

around 50,000 soldiers were dead,

LEARN MORE HERE!

The Union victory at the Battle of Gettysburg was a turning point in the war.

wounded, or missing. Due to the heat,

bodies of the dead were quickly buried.

Many were not given proper burials.

GETTYSBURG INNS

Many places around the town of Gettysburg report paranormal activity, including the inns. The Farnsworth House Inn has as many as 16 different ghosts, from a young boy named Jeremy to several Civil War soldiers. Inn guests have reported the sound of heavy breathing and the feeling of being poked.

A heaviness still hangs in the air around the battlefield and at the gravestones marked "unknown." The feelings of fear and sadness from the battle left their marks on the area. But some visitors experience something more than just a feeling. They have heard and even seen the spirits of the dead.

Civil War veterans of the 40th New York Infantry Regiment reunite at Devil's Den.

Devil's Den is a ridge covered in massive boulders at Gettysburg. This place saw intense fighting on July 2.

Visitors to Devil's Den report their cameras and phones losing battery quickly. They hear the sounds of clanging metal, shouting, and gunfire. Some smell pipe smoke.

There have been several reports of a barefooted, unkempt soldier. He often appears to people who seem lost. He says, "What you're looking for is over there." He always points in the same direction. Witnesses believe the ghost belonged to the 1st Texas Infantry Regiment whose members were known for having ragged clothes.

Battlefield sites tend to feel heavy to visitors, even long after the fighting has stopped.

Jennie Wade was born in Gettysburg in 1843.

While most Gettysburg ghosts are soldiers, the spirit of the only **civilian** to die during the fight is there too. Early on the morning of July 3, Mary Virginia Wade, Jennie for short, was busy baking bread for Union troops. She lived with her sister Georgia in a two-story, red brick house that today serves as a museum.

The sisters were surprised when their

home ended up in the crossfire of the

The brick home where the Wade sisters lived.
The headstone stands in Evergreen Cemetery
on the gravesite of Jennie Wade.

major battle. Instead of fleeing, the Wade women helped and fed soldiers. In the first two days, many bullets hit the home. But on the third day, one penetrated the wood door and hit Jennie as she **kneaded** dough. She died immediately.

Visitors today both see and smell Jennie's spirit. She appears in and around the home. Museum caretakers catch whiffs of her favorite rose-scented perfume. The smell of freshly baked bread fills the home, as if Jennie is still hard at work.

CHAPTER 3
THE LITTLE BAGPIPER BOY

Humans have lived on the hill where

Edinburgh Castle now stands since

850 CE. The castle itself began to take

shape in the 12th century and has since

served as a military **barracks** and royal

residence. Edinburgh Castle is famous for

being one of the most **besieged** castles

COMPLETE AN ACTIVITY HERE!

Edinburgh Castle sits high above Scotland's capital city on Castle Rock.

in the world. So, one can imagine the amount of fighting, torture, and death that took place there.

LADY JANET'S GHOST

Janet Douglas was a Scottish noblewoman accused of witchcraft. She was imprisoned in Edinburgh Castle and later died there in 1537. Today, people see her ghost walking the halls of the castle and weeping.

A few hundred years ago on an August night, tunnels were discovered beneath the castle. One tunnel looked as though it led to Holyroodhouse, located at the bottom of the Royal Mile. People at the castle were curious to explore it, but the entrance was so small that no man could fit. So, they found someone who could.

The Great Highland bagpipe is native to Scotland. It is well known through its use in the British Armed Forces.

Underground tunnels can be found throughout Edinburgh.

A young bagpiper was sent down into the tunnels. He was told to play loudly, so the people could follow him from above. As they all reached Tron Kirk, the piper's music unexpectedly stopped. Search parties gained access to look for the boy but there was no trace of him.

Today, workers and visitors to the castle hear the faint music of bagpipes on occasion. The sound comes from nowhere and everywhere. Perhaps it is the young bagpiper trying to complete his task.

ROYAL MILE AND PATH OF
THE LITTLE
BAGPIPER BOY

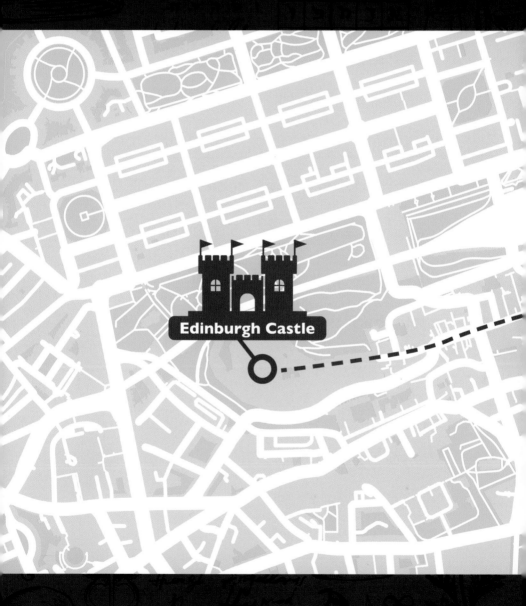

Edinburgh Castle

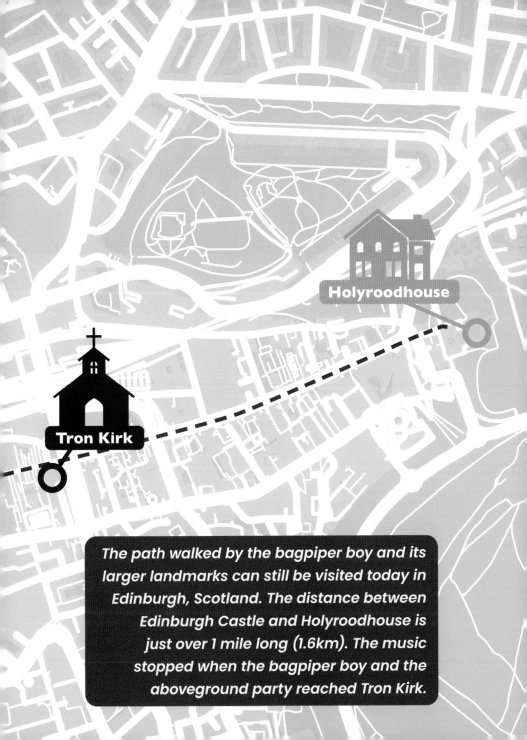

Holyroodhouse

Tron Kirk

The path walked by the bagpiper boy and its larger landmarks can still be visited today in Edinburgh, Scotland. The distance between Edinburgh Castle and Holyroodhouse is just over 1 mile long (1.6km). The music stopped when the bagpiper boy and the aboveground party reached Tron Kirk.

CHAPTER 4

BACK FROM THE DEAD

On May 5, 1957, sisters Joanna and Jacqueline Pollock, ages 11 and 6, walked down the street in their quaint town of Hexham, England. They were suddenly struck and killed by a car. In the following months, the girls' devastated parents,

EXPLORE LINKS HERE!

John and Florence, tried to find happiness again. To the couple's delight, Florence gave birth to identical twin girls on October 4, 1958. They were named Gillian and Jennifer.

The chance of identical twins is around 3 in every 1,000 births.

Florence and John quickly noticed a few strange things about their newborn daughters. The babies had different birthmarks, which is unusual for identical twins. Jennifer had two birthmarks, one on her waist and another on her forehead. These matched a birthmark and scar her late sister Jacqueline had.

DID YOU KNOW? Many major religions, including Hinduism and Buddhism, hold beliefs in **reincarnation**.

Doctors whose research did not concern reincarnation, like Hemendra Banerjee (center), also interviewed the Pollock twins. Dr. Banerjee's work focused on extra sensory perception, or ESP.

When the twins were 3 months old, the family moved away from Hexham. At around two years of age, Gillian and Jennifer began to ask for certain toys. The toys they were referring to were owned by Joanna and Jacqueline. The twins would have no reason to know about them. The parents were even more stunned when the twins called the toys by the names given to them by their older sisters.

Memories of a past life can haunt children. The memories of favorite toys can be comforting.

A view of Market Street in the historic town of Hexham in Northumberland, England.

One day, the family returned to Hexham. The twins pointed out the places their sisters once frequented. The twins recognized their older sisters' school and favorite playground. As cars passed by, the twins panicked as if they knew something awful could happen.

The Pollock sisters' story caught the attention Dr. Ian Stevenson. He was a psychologist who studied unexplained **phenomena**, including children's memories of previous lives. Dr. Stevenson investigated more than 3,000 cases of possible reincarnation. While his work is famous, it did not definitively answer what happens after death.

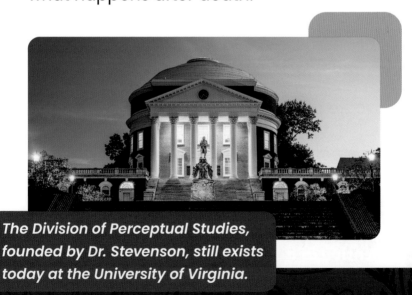

The Division of Perceptual Studies, founded by Dr. Stevenson, still exists today at the University of Virginia.

DR. IAN STEVENSON'S FINDINGS ON REINCARNATION

More than 40 cases verified of the living person having the same scars and birthmarks of the person from the past life

Suspected reincarnated children speak from a very young age

Suspected reincarnated children forget their past life between the ages of 5 and 8

Nearly 40% of parents suppress their children who remember a past life

RIP

Violent death in past life is very common and there is frequent mention of it by the child

MAKING CONNECTIONS

TEXT-TO-SELF

Do you believe it's possible for any of the ghost sightings mentioned in this book to be true? Why or why not?

TEXT-TO-TEXT

Have you read about different religions and what they believe happens after death? Were any of those ideas mentioned in this book?

TEXT-TO-WORLD

Since early times, humans around the world have tried to explain what happens after death. Why do you think that is?

GLOSSARY

barracks — a building or set of buildings where soldiers live for a short amount of time.

besieged — surrounded and attacked by armed forces.

civilian — a person who is not serving in the armed forces or police.

Civil War — specifically the American Civil War, a four-year war (1861-65) between the United States and 11 Southern states that split from the Union and formed the Confederate States of America.

knead — to mix by pressing, folding, and pulling.

phenomenon — an unusual or remarkable person or event.

reincarnation — the religious belief that human souls survive physical death and return in new bodies.

soul — the part of human beings separate from the physical body that is thought of as the center of feeling, thought, and spirit.

theory — a reasonable and sometimes widely accepted explanation for something that happened.

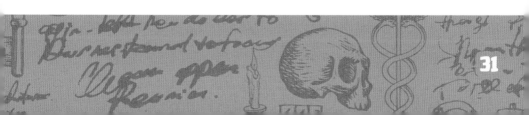

INDEX

ONLINE RESOURCES
popbooksonline.com

Scan this code* and others like it while you read, or visit the website below to make this book pop!

popbooksonline.com/paranormal-events

*Scanning QR codes requires a web-enabled smart device with a QR code reader app and a camera.